"Thank you, Stephan, for giving me the opportunity to own your books or rather your poetry treasure and read it. This evening, I started to read, and as I expected, such beautiful words - a wealth of meanings and a great depth of emotions (and I'm still on the first few pages). I can't wait to read the rest. I'm grateful for the opportunity to indulge in reading books like yours. Your books are going to make my day every time I reach for your words. I read Stephan's poetry every night before I sleep, but I added to it a few minutes of prayer, it gives me calm and fills me with harmony. I don't recite the prayer; I read them from your books. I'm almost done but I shall keep this poetry prayer daily, as I already marked the very special ones to go back to. There are so many to choose from. The feelings and emotions I get from reading Stephan's poems, evokes a cocktail of positive emotions that I can't even describe. Stephan is such a talent and so lucky are those people around him."

HELEN NASRA

"Stephan's poems touch the heart.

BERNADETTE PULEO

"Read Stephan's books! They are breathtakingly spiritual and beautifully written. I can't wait for the next book. Stephan is such a distinguished poet and the books he has written so far are simply beautiful. I read the 1st 110 pages of Stephan's recent book last night and i am in awe of his talent, honesty, and ability to express such heartfelt experiences, and love for Emma, Mia and his entire family. Stephan is creating a legacy for everyone he has touched in life. I'm so grateful to have Stephan as a friend with such a soul. Thank you, Stephan."

JOYCE RIEMER

"Stephan is beyond talented I read and reread his words over and over."

TANYA SENICOLA

"Read his books. They are heartwarming. I love that each poem reads like a short story that is so personal. It's a beautiful escape, so meditative and reminds us of what is important."

ABBY SCHWARTZ

"I am blown away by Stephan's collections of poetry and life advice. They are truly works of art."

DR ROBERT SPENCER

"Stephan has the gift. He seems to know EXACTLY what others need to hear and see to continue paving the way for a happier tomorrow. Stephan's positivity and good heart are admirable."

PAMELA FLORES

"I'm loving Stephan's poetry. I keep the books in my family room and read a few passages any time I take a minute to sit. I absolutely love them!"

MARYANN LANGER

PRAISE FOR STEPHAN SILICH'S POETRY

"Life is a work of art gazing through Stephan's imagination. Stephan's words should be written in the skies."

SINEAD MCGUIGAN
Author of *Unbound, Broken Hearts-Healing Words*
and *My Muse of Restless Nights*

'*this will be the longest night of them all*' is a true gem. I used to resemble beautiful happenings in my life to pearls. These I thread on my necklace of life, which I carry with me all the time. Every free moment I have, I grab for Stephan's beautiful books and read his poetry. I don't know very much about him personally, but somehow it feels like we are tuned in on the same frequency of life's wonderful piece of music. I do think some people exist and some sort of connection between eternity and the present. I'm not a very religious person in a traditional way but I do think there's something more to this world then what we know of. When I'm reading Stephan's books, I'm becoming more convinced we share this situation. I consider Stephan my *soul friend* just through his words."

EVA CHRISTINA NIELSEN
Photographer and author of *Occult*

"Stephan is my favorite writer. Period."

Alex Bilbao

"What happiness must the person feel when receiving these sweet words. They are so wonderful."

JOLS

"Stephan inspires me every single day to pay attention, notice the details, and all our life's simple moments with his poetry. Everyone should read Stephan's poetry to live life well. I thank Stephan for sharing his wisdom so beautifully with us. The world has always needed writers, poets and artists, but perhaps now more than ever. Stephan plays a part in making us feel, remember our shared humanity, and that love really is the only thing that matters. I can't wait to read his next book."

JENNFER BENTLEY

"Stephan's latest collection of writing '*putting the trembling kiss at ease*' kept me engaged well beyond delivering back a timely thank you. *My aching hands* is such a beautiful guidepost for his daughters. For his readers also. Stephan must have such a grounded core to, at all times, see pain through love, beauty in loss, depth in the ordinary. This is a very uplifting collection. The reader learns so much about Stephan, his life, his perspective when reading his writing. Yes, it's the reader who carries on, after the reading, rethinking the rain, noticing the breeze in the curtain, imagining the conversation not had. Thank you, Stephan. One can only put so many layers of paint on old walls. What it takes to return to the beautiful print wallpaper underneath it all is something one doesn't want to think about in the old folks' home. Best to give it a thought now, eh? Thank you for the nudge! And thank you so very much for sharing your writing, your family, and an occasional surprise pop in at the flower shop."

SARAH WRIGHT
Florist and Artist

"Stephan has so much talent and his poems always stay with me, which I love. I never really got poetry until I read his work."

LEAH VITALE

"*Tonight will be longest night of them all* is an amazing read. Everyone should put it on their bedside table and savor it nightly."

NINA FORD RICHTER

"I've been reading Stephan's books, and I mean this, it's been a cleansing for the spirit. I'm connecting with it profoundly. It has me looking at my own work in a new light."

DANIEL ROBERTS

"I really admire how present Stephan is and how he implements gratitude practice in all that he does. His words have helped me maintain perspective and stay positive. I appreciate his honesty and vulnerability in sharing his words with me."

HANNAH FLAM

"I am honored to read Stephan's books, and I am moved immensely by what Stephan has to say and how he made me feel. His works are beautiful words of wisdom."

MARIAN VITALE

"I've started reading Stephan's poetry. I am impressed by his talent. Stephan's ability to convey deep emotions and vivid imagery through his words is remarkable. I am looking forward to diving deeper into Stephan's work and savoring every poem."

HAIDER ALI

"It was 4AM, and I was wide awake because of jet lag, so I started reading *tonight will be the longest one of them all*. The words brought tears to my eyes. I was alone with the words, black tea, warm clothes, and the gentle light in my room. ...Stephan's work has enabled me to travel freely in my mind and to connect to old stories I lived, invented, or lived in another life. Every evening, by opening reading his book, I get just the right moment of peace with myself and for that, my heart and my mind are grateful. Stephan's poems are so impactful and of a precision bordering on brilliance."

RAPHAEL VITRAT

"Stephan books bring me solace."

VICTORIA JASP

"In the evening, I read a few poems when I get in bed. The poems relax me. The words... so beautiful, so detailed... calming my soul and grounding me to the real value of life."

ROBIN SCHECHTER

"And once again, Stephan's poetry expands and unfolds the way sunsets do, unpredictable and brilliant…leaving traces of color in my heart at the end of every word. So very happy for Stephan. He is such a light and so is his new book. It's a privilege to be able to say the quiet part out loud. The fact that Stephan even can is why you must."

JENNIFER FONTAO

ALSO BY STEPHAN SILICH

the silence between what i think and what i say (2018)
tonight will be the longest night of them all (2020)
putting the trembling kiss at ease (2023)
remember me as a time of day (2024)
how impossibly beautiful everything really is (2025)

and
the
flowers
turn
their
faces
toward
the
sun

stephan silich

BROOKLYN
WRITERS PRESS

Copyright 2025 by Stephan Silich

All rights reserved.

Published in the United States of America by the Brooklyn Writers Press, an imprint of Book Biz Hub, LLC

brooklynwriterspress.com

The Brooklyn Writers Press values and supports copyright. Copyright fuels creativity, encourages diverse voices, promotes freedom of expression, and supports a vibrant culture. Thank you for purchasing an authorized edition of this book and for respecting intellectual property laws by not reproducing, scanning, or distributing any part of it by any means without permission. You are supporting authors and enabling the Brooklyn Writers Press to continue to publish books for everyone. No part of this book may be used or reproduced in any manner for the purpose of training artificial intelligence technologies or systems.

In accordance with Article 4(3) of the Digital Single Market Directive 2019/790, the Brooklyn Writers Press expressly reserves this work from the text and data mining exception.

For permissions or information on bulk orders, please contact:
publish@bklynwriterspress.com

ISBNs:
978-1-952991-41-7 (e-Book)
978-1-952991-42-4 (Paperback)
978-1-952991-43-1 (Hardback)

Library of Congress No. 2025919411

First Edition

Cover Photography by Stephan Silich
Cover design by the Brooklyn Writers Press

Printed in the United States of America

again…

for my daughters, emma and mia.
for my brother, robert.
for my parents, robert and dianne.

as always, this is for you.

(dad, i miss you and hope you can still hear me.)

> *"What should we say? How perfect is this.
> How lucky are we."*
>
> — Bench Plaque, Central Park, New York

contents

the splendor of being human 1

am i a poet? 3

ongoingness 5

blueprints 6

when your parents die 7

the secret 9

to live well in one's soul 10

my escape 11

tenderness 12

extended to all 13

don't multitask 14

night 15

self 16

posing 17

gratitude 18

can't remember 19

the best part of every day 20

life is everywhere 21

unknown 22

solitary hymns 23

allow 24

moments 26

always children 27

free 28

prayer 29

nature 30

acceptance 31

my own backyard 32

by my side 34

your eyes 35

the city and the moon 36

enough 37

language 38

live 39

contentment 40

one and only life 41

the morning 42

these words 43

passing 45

when you leave 46

the sweetest hours 47

these words 48

the human heart 49

serious 50

trying 51

the soul 52

united we stand 53

dislike 54

the language of children 55

the portrait 56

a place of shade 57

the night 58

a thousand candles 59

a million tears 60

life 61

the beech tree 62

hope 63

shining with tears 64

a life 65

time 66

possible 67

harmonize 68

waiting for her 69

watch 70

belief 71

all the beauty and the bloodshed 72

trees 74

what is this? 75

emma and sleeping 77

you 79

crucified 80

humans 81

life 82

question 83

poets 84

splendid isolation 85

dying together 86

a visit to my dad's gravesite 87

victory 90

my heart 91

defeated 92

endure 93

the longing 94

evenings and mornings 95

awkward and quiet 96

the underside of flowers 97

morning light 98

my prayers 99

path 100

sigh and shrug 101

hope 102

the miracle of existence 103

alone 104

5th avenue 105

a poem for the girl i didn't talk to 106

august rain 108

mix well 109

bus ride 110

30,000 feet in the clouds 111

false alarm 112

our exhausted collapse 113

every single day 114

exhausted 115

3 bottles of wine 116

wild palms 117

second chance 118

not a good time for you 119

silence 120

mia and the elevator 121

beyond "until death do us part" 122

unfolding graces 123

the difference 124

truth 125

nothing but love 126

time 127

lucky 128

central park and the golden sun 129

endurance 131

transcendent 134

for my publisher 136

finality 139

the final years 140

perkins pancake house 141

stars 144

capable 145

young love 146

mortality 147

the result 150

the miraculous 151

rest 152

the lasts 153

blink 154

still point 156

be 157

hold it first 158

always remain 159

meaningfulness 161

exist 162

my children are my teachers 164

life and time 167

your eyes 168

our small acts 169

last line written 171

you 172

turtle music 173

the sunset 174

the eclipse 175

aliveness 178

count to 10 179

life is better 180

writing 181

burst of emotion 182

sacred feelings 183

immense grace 184

not to be sold 185

wakeful dreaming 186

my day job 187

poetry 189

ordinary things 190

secrecy 192

works of art 193

haunting and comfortable 194

sunset and weeping 195

22,630 days 196

last love 197

hope 198

and the flowers turn their faces towards the sun 199

postscript 2011

A Thankful Poem 2022

Words from Mia 2033

Acknowledgements

About the Author

the splendor of being human

the true splendor of being a human being
is that we are born
and we die as part of nature.

you always have to consider
the totality of your being
and you should always
give a blessing to one's own life.

never fail to reach a hope
or meet an expectation.

it's ok to embrace the perennial
uncertainty of the future,
but you should still marvel
at the passage of time.

forget righteousness,
disregard disapproval from those you do not love,
know the intrinsic value of truth and honor.

know yourself completely.

clarify and sanctify your meaning.

have no ego and no self-image.

don't be inauthentic and disconnected.

be a person of substance,
of flesh and bone.

many will refuse to see you, so what?

don't ever let the so-called critics

and the indifference of humanity
crush your spirit.

live like this and you will always
make it back into your soul.

am i a poet?

i had hoped someone would like my poetry
well enough to give me some encouragement,

and my parents did,
at the young age of 13.

growing up, i had many exposures to beauty,

and i knew i needed a job to be able to create.

i made my day job,
essential to my writing.

the steady paycheck allows me
and these poems to remain a purely creative act.

i hope my poems still
feel small and private.

i want you to read something
that realigns your soul,
and i hope it comes gently.

i write all the time:
on my daily walk to work,
at home in the evenings,
in the car on the weekends…

and this will be
my only participation
in the world
as i know now that the task of midlife
is to stand naked before the world.

i will let my life speak

and hopefully affirm the beauty of art and love.

i will surrender to the imperfections
of human beings

as this imperfect realness
is what true love is based on and built on,

and we are stronger for these imperfections,
and this is the very wellspring of true love.

ongoingness

no love ever fails,
but we get it wrong sometimes.

starting with full hope
and ending with broken pieces,
but holding on
to the remembering
of the everlasting wonder of it

as we keep trying
we keep living
the unstoppable
ongoingness of life
alongside the shadow of time.

blueprints

review those blueprints
for finding a way out of grief,
for there will be those
whom we should hold
for as long as we need.

i don't think
time heals all wounds,
but time never stands still.

we can pray to san lazarus,
the patron saint of healing,
for a little guidance
on how we should respond
to people in pain.

it is heart-tearing work,
but it's a celebration of life.

when we hear music
or poetry
or stories,
the world opens up again.

it's the unveiling of the eyes
where we will use words
to reveal and not conceal
that we do matter,
and so does everyone else.

when your parents die

i was very close to my parents,
and like many people
who loved their parents,
i didn't think i would survive without them,
but somehow you do.

as my father lay dying,
i felt moments of pure tenderness,
even exaltation.

as i glimpsed his death,
i witnessed something
i knew nothing about.

we lose people.
we lose our grandparents.
we lose our parents.

and when your parents die,
you will never be the same.
you might think you understand that,
but until it happens, you don't.

but you will venture
into the unknown
and discover new truths
that are both tender and timeless
and will stay etched into your heart.

ensure that your particular beauty
is inseparable from its fragility,
and allow for tragedy to befall you.

fortunate that we had the love,
i'm grateful that we got to say goodbye.

haunted by loss, saved only by love,
the grand act of our wonderous love

the beating heart of these books
and their gentle pages and notes,

these precious hours,
this bittersweetness,
and the divine serenity of the horizon.

the secret

stop measuring your days
by productivity
and start experiencing them
by presence
because all we have
is the aching beauty
of the passage of time

and maybe a magnificent glimpse of the world
and the gestures of those small flowers
opening in the morning just for you.

to live well in one's soul

read a lot of stories,
listen to a lot of music,
have a willingness to be exposed.

and think about your own life
and the lives of those you love.

and let those you love
sing themselves through you
as you sing yourself
into the longing for life.

my escape

i have escaped
from a world of distractions.

i have been left alone
to read and recite
poetry to the sky.

the unbroken solitude
that has inspired me
keeps me present
in the living world.

and all these
fragments of my heart
remain with you.

tenderness

this life of ours
is losing its everyday tenderness.

yet we need this delicacy
to save us from reality,

and to warm us awake
from just near-living
to make sense of the world
and our place in it.

extended to all

everything that you think
is profoundly attached
is actually fleeting and ephemeral.

but your love reveals
the possibility of the
fragility of humanity.

and the weight of our world,
with its expanding
and deepening emotions,

with its visible
and invisible hands,

are as real as something
that transcends time,
with its own specific texture
and memory of profound reverence,

like our childhood years
of intense beauty and wonder,
and that should now be extended to all.

don't multitask

be here now.

don't let your daily work
dull your mind
and deplete your soul.

devote yourself
to one task at a time,
remembering that
the shortness of our days on earth
is final and delicate.

surrender to the human condition,
accepting the reality of our limitations.

there will always be
more to do,
no matter what you think we finish.

so be here now.

night

during the beauty
and splendor
and poetry of night,
when my words seem to come alive,

i am able to recollect
the day's joys and sorrows

and stay ablaze with hope
to grasp again the human heart,

for it is the miracle of love
that defeats time.

self

embrace what they criticize in you
and what they don't like about you.

keep that going,
nurture it,
that's precisely
what makes you an individual.

posing

posing
is the enemy,
in writing
and
in life.

gratitude

hold the possibilities in both hands
between us and within us.

learn to sing the songs of life.

widen the boundary of your being.

write your love letters to the memories of trees
and this will remain in your book of days.

stay away from
the controlling ones,
the conquering ones,
and the competitive ones.

they break the world.
they cause war.
they destroy human beings.

awaken the compassionate awareness
and the urgency of your existence.

bear witness to the world.

fill your heart with uncontainable gratitude.

the graces of aging,
the delicacy of the soul,
and the reflections of nature
will always be within reach.

can't remember

i think of that time now,
and the years after:

you were the place i can't remember
and the place i can't forget.

the best part of every day

the constant force in this human life
is my genuine, gentle love for you both
and the endless rewards that i have been given
to my heart, my mind, and my spirit.

the sweetness of our hopes
is also the secret language of night
when our words fade a little
and when the love returns
and resembles the beautiful love given.

you are the architecture of my existence
and the pure art of living.

i don't think when i'm with you;
i just feel.

and it's a cathedral of emotion
wrapped in wonderous magic,
and it's the best part of every day.

life is everywhere

what remains
between good people
is only love.

live with a tender heart;
keep it gentle and gracious;

and let humanity radiate
as a testament to
an all-eclipsing cherishment of life

and a vivid reminder of the wonderful way
the world holds us.

our love is simply a gentle reminder
not to let go of a single moment of our living.

unknown

the anguish of others
in the midst of our own
because everyone will have
a last day with you

and no one will know
when that will be.

solitary hymns

these words,

these solitary hymns,

born from the silent places

i can only hope to lend
the unnamable some truth
and reveal this still beating heart

to stay present,

to pay attention,

and to love the world
a little more.

allow

allow your mind
to wander,
to daydream,
to find a precious memory.

allow the soft light of love
to fall upon you.

allow your soul to be treated
with a great deal
of gentle attentiveness.

allow the certitude of love
to bring the expressive hours.

allow for sleep and wakefulness
beneath the shadow of old trees.

allow yourself to sit quietly
and let the moments unfold
as the overwhelming cruelty
of this world surrounds us.

allow your intimate, private portrait
to be painted over and over again.

and allow yourself
the realization that you will lose
everything and everyone you cherish.

so you need to love more fully
and live more deeply,

magnifying each and every day

as you bear witness to one another
forever locked in your eternal loving embrace.

moments

we will of course have beautiful moments,
but we will also have some not so beautiful moments.

but the remembrance and the guide
is to always know that we had moments.

and the moment i'm writing this,
it's springtime.

and now is the opening of flowers and trees,
reminding us that life is livable.

then they stop blooming
to remind us that life must be lived.

always children

we are the same now
as our childhood selves,
and that is the perpetual miracle
always alive in each of us.

it is our integrity of identity,
and no matter how much changes

we are still that person
looking through the lens
at the sacredness of smallness
to the majesty and mystery of life

and the eternity of a single moment
pressed close against the next.

free

i said it before:

all art should be free.

poetry and art suffers
the moment people start paying for it.

prayer

serenely waiting for sleep

it is the quietness that is beautiful
and almost unbearable.

the stillness is my eternal prayer.

nature

birds flying in unison
without colliding,
thousands of them

the astounding grandeur
of these small, fragile creatures.

i look up and the silence
stretches across the sky,
and nothing can change this beautiful hour.

and then there are
the mountains,
the rivers,
the stones,
and the slow shifting of earth.

it is here
that this summer evening
preserves our innocence,
and it is here
where i have fallen in love with you.

i hold your heart with both hands.

i see you with both eyes.

let's wrap ourselves
in a night of sleep
under careful stars,

and we will be left
with whispers of immortality.

acceptance

i will try not to scream
when
it comes,

accepting the moment
like a man
spreading out
on a field of grass
to take in the afternoon sun

my own backyard

i prefer my own backyard
to almost any other place
in the world.

it is here that i can
watch the moon rise
and traverse the sky,
giving insight into the
life of my heart.

looking up to look inward.

it is the solemn opportunity
to escape spiritually
and hold on to the
strength of sensitivity.

here, it feels like
earth is resting
and i am at home
with the silence of the world.

here is beauty that didn't have to exist,
but does now with a piercing elegance.

our very presence here is a blessing.

and we continue this blessing
with the awareness of being human

and keeping our shining eyes
radiating with love
as we try to inspire
and celebrate wonder
between each of us and one another.

and i will keep coming here
every weekend
because i always
take the way home
that leads back to
the recollections and
remembrances.

by my side

with you by my side
i no longer have to ask
who am i and where should i go?

your eyes

i see the generous light in your eyes,

the quiet light of your heart
that mirrors and magnifies your soul,
a lot like the silence of trees.

they cast a shimmering radiance
that borders on majestic,
like the stars,
shining eternally.

my days of solitude
are filled with thoughts of you.

let's take a walk at sundown,
unhurried by the falling light.

let's expose our naked hearts,

let's cling to each other,
full of desperation and dreams,

let's make promises to keep,

and let's allow our love to triumph
as we grow very old together.

the city and the moon

this city is empty
save you and i,
so i will steal away
to meet you
when the moon is full.

let's join
our solitary completeness of being
and our private souls.

enough

the street corners,
the madhouses,
the landlords,
the bruised knuckles,
the unfinished poems,

i ask nothing of you
but enough time
to just finish what i've started.

language

our search for meaning.

our need for beauty.

our tender lives that are worth living.

we need

our language of words,
beauty,
music,
kindness,
flowers,
tenderness,
harmony,

our language of light,

and of course our language of love.

live

as we witness
our lives now,
full of perpetual distraction
and information saturation,

we cannot allow this
to compromise our humanity.

we need to stay
more interested in feelings
than events and happenings.

we know what we have to endure to make a living.

we know what we have to do to feel alive.

do not let them extract money
out of your blood and bones.

do not listen to the noise
and inducements of every waking hour
to be something you are not.

take a turn if you have to
and run toward
the possibilities of the unknown.

look for the exceptional moments.

be a testament to forgiveness.

and remember,
you are the deepest part of me.

please always remember us this way.

contentment

through the voice of poets
and the echo of hearts

our complete contentment
is the last triumph.

one and only life

i think of her
and realize it was
the quietness
of her departure
that broke me.

but life discovers us
and i'm no longer at war
with the world that
won't let me in.

and so
among the empty storefronts
and soaped over windows,
i make choices in a city of chaos
while remembering
behind the nervous laugh
is often the terrible cry.

but these anthems to love,
loss, and yearning
are how we try to show each other
what it is like to be alive,

and what will relieve the human heart
in the midst of our one and only life.

the morning

waking up to wakefulness
is the key to live a divine day.

most wake ready for labor
but very few wake for poetry.

these words

staggeringly timely resonance
as we linger,
walking back and forth.

this living miracle
is a temporary miracle,
answered by your eyes
before they are answered
by your words.

don't step on someone's toes
and don't stand on their shoulders.

forget jealousy and don't covet
what somebody else has
that is the surest way
to forfeit your uniqueness.

i stretch out on the bed
staring upward, following the
patterns of sunlight on the ceiling.

it is quiet here in my room,
where i have these thoughts
and where i write these words.

words that weaken me
and try to crush me
with their importance,

but these moments turn into pages
as life remains,
the little cry weeping
for a little more time
and for another chance

to turn it all around.

passing

the years
are passing by
in an eyeblink,
but that is because
life is being lived.

when you leave

every time you leave,
i still see you
through the falling leaves
and the fading sunlight.

i am screaming inside,
but no one can hear me.

you simply take the air out of my lungs.

i disregard the tales of lyrical loneliness
as i search for one final gesture of generosity.

and it's this unassailable love,
emanating echoes through
warm afternoon breezes,
that ennobles the human spirit,
and shapes the quality of our lives.

my astonished ache-etched face
will shine through
these genuine moments
of emotional dignity
as time changes
in the dwindling of this day.

these shadows will help us embrace
the winding trails of life
as we make art and poems and songs.

all hiding in plain sight,
but still learning to love.

the sweetest hours

my heart is always in the way,
but these are the sweetest hours
of affection

because i believe in memory
and in carrying you in my heart,
past the unrelenting absence
and impermanence of this
one and only life.

these words

written with courage and openheartedness,
honoring the truth and beauty of the world,
hopefully some of these words
will be a parting gift to all humanity.

all we can do is try to live
with an aching awareness
and a terrifying clarity
of the irreducible experience
of being alive.

the pace of our history
and the urgencies of our own time
require us to accept the invitation
to a more radiant world
filled with my enchanting experiences
of nature, music, and love.

the very things that
move the clouds and illuminate the stars.

once you have this clear lens
on beauty and on wonder,

the transcendent will arrive
for you every day,
forevermore,
and the infinite will remain.

the human heart

the unfailing human heart,
much like a last breath,
enters the soul
and remains there
with quiet dedication
as a heartwarming
and heartbreaking
eternal exhale.

serious

being serious
is not easy
in our modern society.

but we need to let others know
that we are present for them,
that we will try to understand.

we need to see things
that go unseen and unnoticed,
the things others might prefer
not to notice.

we need to remain
interconnected and intertwined
along with the meaning
and the measure of this evolution
of our life.

we need to not be burdened
by the towering highs
and crushing lows
and allow the ennobling
of our humanity
to honor those we have lost,
so we can carry the weight
of our love together.

and we need to hold
boundless tenderness
for all these moments,
always
amid the overwhelming
cruelty of this world.

trying

i keep trying to find our heaven
right here in this beautiful
and troubled world.

i keep trying to stay openhearted
to the tenderness of this life

and what it really means to be alive,
as all of our moments are imprinted
with the voice of stillness
and the awareness that
staying present is sacred.

i accepted the invitation to a forgotten way
of seeing the world many years ago
and it has haunted me all my life.

the questions that live in me
and the brief time given to me
illuminate my priorities and passions,
and my love for you
will remain as vast as space
and as deep as the tapestry of night.

the soul

to sit with a loved one
as they lie dying
is an act
of profound courage
and pure braveness.

it is the soul
longing for the impossible,
as we finally realize
we are only saved by love
and it's the infinite in us all.

united we stand

on a flight from new york
to cabo san lucas
for our annual family easter vacation

the captain comes on the loudspeaker and askes:

   "are there any anniversaries on the plane?"

my ex says:

   "yes, it's the anniversary of our divorce."

nervous laughter rings out
and then the steward comes over to me and says:

   *"this is on me.
   here's some baileys
   for your coffee…
   and by the way,
   it's amazing
   what you are doing
   for your children."*

i smiled and said thank you
and returned to the movie
i was watching,
and at that very moment
our wedding song comes on the tv…

dislike

i will always disdain
our culture's worship of status

the sadness of celebrities

the hollow and the callousness
of compulsive achievement.

but remember,
your breaking point
may just be the next portal of possibility.

the language of children

part ode,
part elegy,

with deep meaning,
deep simplicity,
and deep sincerity,

the words of children
are the gifts of wonder,
gratitude, and pure grace.

the portrait

as the portrait of life unfolds
with its joys and sorrows,
the mystery of life is put upon us,
with its shifting seasons
at the edge of all possibility.

we hold an abiding affection
for each other,
built on tenderness,
equanimity, and a sense of joy.

like the whispered fables,
we read to our children in the dark.

this is our source of wonder

and our searching souls
continue with kind eyes.

a place of shade

i will spend
the rest of my days,
from the very beginning
to the end of sleep,

looking for a place of shade
to read the secrets of your heart.

the night

as the sun begins to set,
i welcome the uncertainty.

letting the night,
undulating and unfolding,
change us
as we surrender to the process
like dried flowers,
the eternal symbol
of the passage of time.

it is here where love takes hold
as the birds gather in groups,

and we remember that
love has gentle hands
and i hold them both for you.

a thousand candles

angels breathe leaves from trees
and exit, beating wings across this century.

here, the ache often
turns into joy
because of the short distance
to your heart
from the outside world,

and because you unshaded the sun
while wrapping my hands with rosaries.

this is matched only by the
breathing between us.

and it is here
that your smile remains
like a thousand candles
crushing darkness,
making life
decently bearable.

a million tears

if caught at the right moment,
we are all beautiful
and all worth a million tears.

life

life is exquisitely enriched and ennobled
by the basic humanity of being capable of joy.

and with this,
we can live honorable and generous lives,
lives of beauty and substance.

where we only add
to the wonder of the world
and never subtract from it.

the beech tree

we admire our tree's generosity,
kindness, and thoughtfulness.

its wordless willingness
to care for us
by creating a space of beauty,
a place of shade,
and a safe harbor around her.

she gives us our sense of sanctuary
as we continue to live with her
with attention and due care.

through the summer's haze of blooming
and the winter's veil of bare branches.

hope

pass me on the street
and i will watch you walk away
until my eyes squint no longer.

i hope you turn around.

i hope you come back.

and i hope you think about me
when you return home,
and lie down on your side.

shining with tears

what is unwritten,
what is unfinished,
what is uncertain,
is only the symphony of the possible
and the grace of beginning.

it is the world that awaits you.
so live now,
eyes shining with tears

a life

weary inside
but with glimmers of grace
holding alongside
the remnants of the falling sky
as we continue with
the daily act of living.

don't ever worry
about the lives
you were unable to live.

the life you have chosen to live
is what makes you who you are,
with your beautiful sense of self.

in your being is the marvelous inheritance
of your inner heart

and the remembrance
of your time and space,

with its beginning and its ending.

time

when we were together
time moved differently,
and we let love continue,
lastingly.

possible

the birth of the world
and its brutal beauty
is disquieting sometimes,
like a requiem for a life
that has passed.

and now it all remains
like a lost dream,
with a quiet consolation
for an echo of time when
children laughed,
lovers took an afternoon nap,
flowers flourished,
the elderly held hands,
and poetry was possible.

harmonize

let's harmonize
into something beautiful,
where each of our singularities
intimately survives the other
with an unrelenting spirit
to become the unsurprising
testament to hope
and the courage of love.

waiting for her

it's a journey she has chosen
to make on her own
and now someone else
will be waiting for her
with open arms
at her beautiful destination.

but i will always have
our first days together.

i will remember how the hours
marked the beginning of those days
and how they healed the wounds
from the previous ones.

i stayed to hold her hand,
but she never reached for it.

it was heaven just a moment ago,
but i had it all wrong.

i am left with the heartbreak
and heroism of love,
just an echo of a memory now.

yet i still can't help but think
that the gods are kind

and living now in this expanded way
will only bring uncontainable gratitude.

watch

unload the trucks.
pour the drinks.
pass the food.

watch women whose blouses are too low.
watch men whose skin looks too soft.
watch both laugh much louder than you can stand.

clean up empty glasses.
throw out half-eaten food.
reload the trucks.

walk home knowing
the hollywood version is always a lie.

beware of those who give off
a really good first impression
and remember that no one
really lights up a room.

so crawl into bed tonight
and wake tomorrow to end
the unending tragedy of false existence
by affirming the resilience of life
and the essence of what it means to be human.

belief

the tears i cry
are all i believe.

all the beauty and the bloodshed

i see the hungry,
the disregarded,
the bruised bodies,
the bared souls.

i will extend to you the comforting care
i am unable to grant myself.

i know of the beautiful gifts
of kindness and mercy
that human beings can give one another.

i know at some point,
from the sea to the stars,
the earth will become
abandoned to darkness
and the universe will become
desolate for the rest of time.

don't let the world diminish
and reduce what you think and feel.
it is words that count in the end,
in the beginning,
in all time.

words spoken softly
through the unimaginable vastness of time,
which makes aging and death inevitable
but awakens the pure pleasure of existing
as the days pass uncounted,
with each moment unrecoverable,
each memory wrapped in warmth.

for now
i see the exceptionally graceful stars

silently gathering to be our lights home,
as our hearts stay achingly intimate
and invigoratingly hopeful

with all the bruises that never heal,
and all the beauty
and the bloodshed.

trees

the trees hold memories
and they hear all that's left to be heard
and all that is left unsaid.

what is this?

the nature of grief
can stretch and compress time
and reshape common memories
and trials endured.

this is neither the end of civilization
nor the rebirth of humanity;
it's just the breath of this immense world.

there are those who give
and those who take.

let's focus on those who give.

and let them give us
love,
hope,
art,
literature,
family,
children,
memories.

they are with us
in half-remembered dreams
and wind-swept ocean breezes.

they give us the ache,
but also the astonishment.

they give us the sorrow,
but also the beauty.

they don't allow
the pain of despair

to be insurmountable.

they prevent us
from suffering
the long, slow passing
of the soul.

they give us silence

like the flowers and the moon.

they keep our hearts,
textured and timeworn.

and they let us live
from stardust to stardust
across the unrelenting
beautiful aliveness of life.

emma and sleeping

in the hush of night, we lay together,
waiting for nightfall
and waiting for the moon
to cast its light with gentle grace
and make the urgency of life fall away.

we share our space with every breath
as we sleep in peace, wrapped in love.

with dreams of tomorrow
as night quietly fades to dawn,

we will greet the world with full hearts
and give the day something of the eternal.

as we live here,
i know the moon is outside my window
reminding us of how lucky we are to exist

and to be here now with this light
that urges us to do nothing
but sit in awe and love each other.
in the hush of night,
we lay together,
waiting for nightfall
and waiting for the moon
to cast its light with gentle grace
and make the urgencies of life fall away.

we share our space with every breath
as we sleep in peace, wrapped in love.

with dreams of tomorrow
as night quietly fades to dawn,

we will greet the world with full hearts
and give the day something of the eternal.

as we live here,
i know the moon is outside my window
reminding us of how lucky we are to exist

and to be here now with this light
that urges us to do nothing
but sit in awe and love each other.

you

the weight of the sun
the glow of the moon…

and you
sleeping in the night,
is the most beautiful sight of all.

crucified

the weight of these years
and my tired eyes

the open wounds
in need of passionate mercy

the words
that have become a salve to my longing

to our song of songs,
with its own melody,
its own lyrics,
and its own verses of rapture
standing still with christ,
crucified between 2 criminals.

the evocation of hope,
the bold beauty of life,
and the declarations
that decrease the distance between us
are my labor of love.

these small words of thought
are nothing more than
a self-portrait of humanity
floating through my bones
and whispering through my blood
shouting at all the blooming
possibilities within us.

humans

humans,
the only ones
who can cry,

the only ones
with knowledge of our end,

the only ones
able to take song
to soaring heights
and melancholy lows,

the only ones
with so many secrets
waiting to be revealed,

the only ones
who can lift each other
above the calamities,

the only ones
who will remember
loneliness happens to you
and solitude happens for you,

the only ones
who will hold you
as close as a memory,

and the only ones
who will love you until the end
and still burn bright for you.

life

life still splits my heart
with its breathtaking beauty.

question

don't the gossip columnists
and so-called journalists,
by reporting exclusively
on the successes and excesses
of the rich and famous,
attempt to undermine the worth of all others?

please remember,
the life in all of us
is worthy of a poem.

poets

poets fall in love
and they fall apart,

and then they fall in love again,
and write about it.

splendid isolation

the splendid isolation that follows
makes the views grander
and the promises deeper.

the sun begins to rest,
the city night emerges,
the traffic lightens,
the sounds grow quieter,
and the breeze rises elegantly
to swallow our souls.

we stay apart from most
except for the small,
humble, and noble
percentage of the human race.

dying together

maybe we will both die together,
in our sleep,
on the same day.

maybe even at the same time.

with arms folded across our chests,
eyes closed,
so neither of us
has to face the world
without the other.

a visit to my dad's gravesite

we went to visit my dad's gravestone in florida,
me, my mom, and my 2 daughters.

we walked the silent ground
in this sacred resting place
to the site, with both emma and mia's
little hands grasping mine very tightly.

emma was first, and she tenderly
placed her hand on top of the stone
and then knelt down in front,
lowered her head, put her hands in prayer form,
and said words that only she could hear.

then it was mia's turn.
she placed both her arms around the gravestone
and gave it a big hug with her arms outstretched.
she started to cry and bowed her head.
she too, said a prayer.

then it was my turn.
i said a prayer to myself:

> "dad, i miss you more than anything.
> i think about you every day and i am
> doing my best to honor your life
> with all the kindness and compassion
> i can find inside. i love you more than anything
> and i really miss you. i hope you can still hear me."

i then took a small patch of soil from his grave
and put it in a baggy so i could take part of his spirit
home with me to new york.

i looked at my mom.

there were tears streaming down her face.

we walked back to the car, and as we were getting in,
mia, my youngest daughter, jumped back out
and ran back to the gravestone and gave it a last hug.

she was crying,
but we know now that your spirit
rests in every tear
and in every laugh with love anew.

we went to visit my dad's gravestone in florida,
me, my mom, and my 2 daughters.

we walked the silent ground
in this sacred resting place
to the site, with both emma and mia's
little hands grasping mine very tightly.

emma was first, and she tenderly
placed her hand on top of the stone
and then knelt down in front,
lowered her head, put her hands in prayer form,
and said words that only she could hear.

then it was mia's turn.
she placed both her arms around the gravestone
and gave it a big hug with her arms outstretched.
she started to cry and bowed her head.
she too, said a prayer.

then it was my turn.
i said a prayer to myself:

> *"dad, i miss you more than anything.*
> *i think about you every day and i am*
> *doing my best to honor your life*

with all the kindness and compassion
i can find inside. i love you more than anything
and i really miss you. i hope you can still hear me."

i then took a small patch of soil from his grave
and put it in a baggy so i could take part of his spirit
home with me to new york.

i looked at my mom.
there were tears streaming down her face.

we walked back to the car, and as we were getting in,
mia, my youngest daughter, jumped back out
and ran back to the gravestone and gave it a last hug.

she was crying,
but we know now that your spirit
rests in every tear
and in every laugh with love anew.

victory

the victory of love
is in the truth and braveness
of coming together for a time.

always a finite time.

always a fleeting moment.

always the now

with the heart still beating
before letting go
with equal truth and braveness
to shape eternity
as we stand with our faces to the sun.

my heart

even though my heart's thread has come undone,
pushing it further into a precarious existence,

it will still confront the fundamental question
of its survival, and remain committed
to the intensely personal feeling of infinity
so that within the bounds of the universe we know,
great love stories can begin again.

there will be more stories.

there are always more stories
to remember and reflect upon
with a singular vulnerability
among the trees and under the stars,
and straight to the renewal
of our spiritual and human closeness.

defeated

the key
is to capture all this
through words

without being defeated
by those who made you write them
in the first place.

endure

losing you at a distance,
no in-person conversation,
no holding your hand,
no thank you,
no parting words of goodbye.

slowly moving away
from the adjacency of this
and the floating melancholy.

i speak in hushed tones,
longing for just a touch.

awash in unease,
howling into the void,

words filled with sighs,
lines filled with aches.

i will hold on
to the capacity for art and hope
and delight in the world
as i pass the time of day
in the wake of dreaming improbable dreams.

through moments of remembrance,
i will still endure what seems unendurable.

the longing

through poetry and prayer,
i search for the recognition of the place
between no more and not yet.

the elemental truth
is that heartache drips
from these words i write for you.

every loss reveals
what we are made of,
and the sorrow weaves
through the tapestry of meaning.

there is great solace to be found here,

in the small acts of quiet courage,

the sense of wonder that comes from stillness,

the richness of mind and the sweetness of temperament,

the divine affection of the purest purpose,

the burning sunsets that draw us close,

the endless reflections and echoes of love,

and the lump in my throat from the longing
to live in a more beautiful world
than the one we live in now.

evenings and mornings

for one undiminished moment of misplaced time,
i saw the inexhaustible flash in your eyes.

we arrived at the museum of our awakening,
and the auguries of loss and aging and passing
were gathered and put away.

sleep will reassuringly elude us tonight,
as our love washes through the stillness
over time,
over dinners,
over books,
over photographs,
over music,
and over evenings
and mornings…

and evenings again
and mornings again.

awkward and quiet

it's the awkwardness and quietness
that is most endearing.

it is a refined representation
of limitless possibility,
and it will make me fall in love with you
over
and
over
and
over
again.

the underside of flowers

the anguish is upon me
as i wash the clothes,
clean the apartment,
cook the food,
drain the sink,
scrub the toilet,
iron the shirts,
park the car,
and walk to work.

it is where i scream at the buildings
through the night,
without ever raising my voice.

it is the underside of flowers.

there is no choice but to stay put
and try to make a life,
a good life,
out of all the ruins.

ruins are the gift.

but this will be my place
of refuge and reflection.

and i will pray for
the conversion of our hearts
as i hurtle toward old age.

morning light

all we have,
as poets
trying to write,
is time to reflect.

we live with our memories,
the beauty and the terror,
and draw rapture from all of it-
equally telling in quieter moments,
and equally more profound
than ever could be imagined.

the empty sheet of paper is yearning still
for the words that mute the rising sun.

i will continue to say no
to requests of my time and energy
and never follow the crowd.

i will push forth with
whatever morning light
there may still be left
to radiate and illuminate us.

my prayers

these words are my prayers.

i am talking to you through these pages.

the better parts of me
are found right here in these books.

all that i am
is in these poems,
which have to fit inside this envelope
that i will send to only you.

path

the path your life cuts through the world
should have its greatest impact
on those you love and those who love you.

like a good poem,
a piece of music,
a park bench,
a sense of tranquility,
a final confession,
and a bedtime story.

only a word
only a passing minute
only a whisper
only a glance
only a touch

it should all linger…

sigh and shrug

if attention happens to come your way
and the critics are laudatory,
sigh.

and if the critics are disparaging,
shrug.

creation will bear witness.

keep a dignified composure
and an attentive aliveness
and serenity through it all,
and especially as you approach the great sleep
with full awareness of your mortality.

how you conduct yourself matters-
through birth, love, and death.

and remember,
there is always light somewhere,
even in the cracks.

hope

i do this
to keep my words from fading
and to have a small share
in the whole of human destiny.

i vowed to stay
incandescently honest
and to fully wrap my arms
around the limits of my existence
and the fact that
we are all temporary.

but maybe this is the hope i needed,
because i think
i've said too much now
in these books.

but then again,
maybe i haven't said enough.

the miracle of existence

the winter season is upon us,
and as the leaves are lost
our bare bones are revealed.

but if you look closely
at the branches,
they are covered in tiny buds
waiting for spring to flower
and reveal the wounds
that we inflicted upon it.

it is the miracle of existence,
like falling in love again.

alone

i find peace
in small rooms
staring at the ceiling
as the light from outside
pierces through and shines
filling up the bedroom
here, i will wait for you
with pressed flowers between pages,
shards of perfume glass,
and words written on torn paper.

i will wait for you,
and the weeping will soon end.

5th avenue

a girl with a handful of flowers
stands at the well-lit subway station
of 5th avenue.

before the platform sings with trains,
she sings these words over and over:

> *"i want to wrap my arms around you...
> but i hope my heart can take it."*

a poem for the girl i didn't talk to

on sunday,
i walked past the small
tables of the outdoor restaurant
and noticed only you.

i looked at you, and
you immediately became
part of my dream.

i continued on,
but the memory of you
burned with sweet anguish.

when twilight fell,
swallowing fields of wildflowers,
i saw you again outside the movie theatre
and dreamed of you again.

my trembling hands reach for you now,
but like the early hours of morning,
you are gone.

i will dream of you again.
i will see you again,
perhaps even have a word with you.

but for now,
i pull the sheets over my face
and sleep with the world's
loneliest companion,
regret.

stretched upon this night,
i remain empty
as this poem nears its end,

but it will be difficult
because somewhere,
at this very moment,

there is a single tear
crawling and burning
down the face of an old man.

august rain

in this august rain
we celebrate our first morning together.

beneath the dripping umbrella,
i stare at your face
and you are unfailingly beautiful.

our day closes with earth
again warning us
that eternity trembles
like the wings of a butterfly.

mix well

listening to schubert on the radio,
clothes in the dryer rumbling
in the background.

the two mix surprisingly well.

my brother lies on one couch
reading a 1,439-page surgical textbook;
i sit on the other
reading a new book by charles bukowski.

the two mix surprisingly well.

1:47a.m.
nowhere to go.
nothing to do.

this is more beautiful
than i could ever have imagined.

bus ride

on a bus downtown
i listen as two girls
talk about cafes and sunsets
and places hemingway
used to drink and write.

i look away
and decide to focus my attention on
the world outside the windows.

just before my stop,
i see an empty parking lot
with a sign for silk flowers.
and then i see
an elderly woman waving her arms,
yelling that life is worth the struggle.

i decide to stay on the bus
and return home quietly,

hoping all of this
will soon be a remembrance
to live with.

30,000 feet in the clouds

reading *notes from the underground*
on an airplane
30,000 feet in the clouds.

i'm thinking
of sitting on the side of my bed
saying prayers to my loved ones
as blood pumps through my human spirit.

i'm thinking
of humanity
and how people waste so much time
being constantly productive
and not being present.

i'm thinking
of summer
and how it seemed so much longer last year.

and now
i'm thinking
that i will try to never allow myself
to be defeated by the weight of this life.

false alarm

9:39p.m.
saturday,
on the subway heading uptown
reading jack kerouac's *desolation angels*.

3 kids get on and immediately crowd in front of me.
i'm sitting; they're standing.

i close the book and wait.

i stare at the 6 legs in front of me,
disguised by blue jeans 4 times too big.

i stare at the 6 hands and watch for
any quick movements,
sharp objects, or any flashes of silver.

i briefly look up and look away.

i notice one look at another and shake his head.
false alarm.

they move away and get off at the next stop.

i return to kerouac,

his words now more wondrous than ever,
and so too will be the rest of my night.

our exhausted collapse

we lie together
until our exhausted collapse
arrives like a moment undone.

our night will tremble before morning
and before the gravedigger
arrives with armloads of flowers,
confirming the worthiness of life.

every single day

in a world where we confuse
hype with achievement,
gossip with history,
money with culture,
and nationality with class,

all we can do is find the humility
to experience every single day.

find something sacred.

something bigger than you.

surrender to the sweep of nature
while not passing through this life
without enjoying all of its hidden blessings.

and always continue to see this life
through the eyes of your love
and memorialize it.

exhausted

march 23, 2021
2:24am.

lying in bed
thinking how the sun
will someday bow her head
and become quiet
as though she has
completely exhausted herself.

i will lie here and weep with joy,
because in this cruel world,
my heart still drools for life.

3 bottles of wine

as this century's end
shivers to a close,
the moment finds us—
2 men,
2 women,
and a night of rain.

one man reads the poetry of the other
while speaking about the poetry
of his own life
and how a wave hello from a lone farmer
on the wheatfields of delaware
changed his course under the brave sun.

as time pushes forth,
with 3 bottles of wine,
tears come with words;
courage with silence.

upon leaving this night,
we are left with the memory
of strong hands holding a small book
and knowing that tomorrow
the flowers will try even harder.

this, i am sure of.

wild palms

the days pass
one night, then another
as we lie together in bed
remembering how
we used to sit on that bench
surrounded by wild palms
falling
in
love
over
and
over again.

second chance

as laughter froze in the throats of time,
your silence stretched into a fragile smile,
and words arrived like a child's touch:

> *"the most beautiful thing in life*
> *is a second chance."*

my heart widened and whispered:

> *"may the saddest days of your future,*
> *be the happiest days of your past."*

not a good time for you

i knew this girl once.
we worked together for a catering company.
she liked to read rilke
and drink wine
and live a quiet life,
so i asked her out for dinner
and she said:
    "it's not really a good time for me."

we lost contact
for about a year and a half,
and when we reconnected,
she now talked about
being a famous actress,
how she liked to pose naked
for fashion photographers,
and how she lived with this guy
who paid her rent.

this time, she asked me out for dinner
and i said:
    "i guess it's still not a good time for you"

she sat there in stunned silence,
and i walked away
into the early parts of the night
with my soul beautifully intact.

silence

i look at you across from me
in that restaurant and realize:

when faced with that kind of beauty,
all you can do is stay still
and watch the light from the fireplace
achingly illuminate
everything that you are to me.

mia and the elevator

my 9-year-old daughter,
my little mia,
and her guiding hand,
in the quiet hours of night,
walking me to the elevator
every time i am ready to leave for the night.

it is our moment to bind our hearts together

in this sweet ritual
filled with warmth and love
as we stand by the elevator door.

with a hug and a kiss
we say goodnight to another day
and find the courage to carry on.

she says: *"i love you, dad."*
i say: *"i love you more."*
she says: *"never."*
i say: *"always."*

as the doors close,
we have our silent exchange of love
and our everlasting beacon of hope for tomorrow.

beyond "until death do us part"

i know a part of me
will belong to this earth
somewhere, somehow,
whether through my human spirit
or through the ashes of my remains.

and because of that,
the earth and myself
will always remember you,

and always love you.

unfolding graces

expect nothing from this world
and you will be given daily victories,
which in turn lead to many
spiritual rewards of gratefulness
among life's unfolding graces.

living with uncertainty,

embracing the unfamiliar,

allowing for not knowing,

permitting us to not be sure,

living the questions,

being thankful for small mercies,

staying wakeful at all times,

and remembering
that the practice of kindness and love
is the centerpiece of a full life.

the difference

know the difference
between false work
and the true work of your life.

you can first reshape your world
by surrendering to it all,
living independently of the external,

i will keep the essential humanness
of what a human being is meant to be.

i will never sleep.

i will never leave.

and i will love you
until my last breath
and beyond,
until eternity.

truth

the one fragment
of truth i know
is that love
and remembrance
are now inside me
and can never be lost.

despite life's meditation
on mortality and evanescence,
this will stay,
always.

nothing but love

amid the ticking of the clock
the moments are among us
like the evening spread out
against the sky
in the dim twilight
where past and future blend together.
and life abounds,
as each heartbeat echoes fleeting days,
but each story is a step
through these timeworn streets.

in the quiet,
in the pause,
the beauty of life is found.

a whisper through the shadows,
the pulse of existence,
a moment borrowed.

a reflection on life's brevity,
where time and memory meet,
and i will write this in the ink of ages,
where each heartbeat becomes a stanza,
and each breath becomes a verse.

even at the edge of life,
there's peace in these silent tones.

and in your embrace,
all the wrongs feel right.

and in twilight's grasp,
we may have a last goodbye
that will be wrapped in nothing but love.

time

we are made of time

the substance of our minutes,

the substance of our lives,

both intimate and visible.

and what we do with that time
is our expression of love
through lived presence,
and attention,
and devotion.

lucky

if we are lucky,
a few times in our lifetime
we will encounter

a work of art,

a moment in nature,

a great poem,

a wonderful song,

and a great love
that we will feel immediately
and that will exist outside of time .

central park and the golden sun

in central park,
where lovers roam beneath blue skies,
i walk with my 2 daughters.

hand in hand
we stroll amid nature's embrace,
and our family tree remains a bond
that cannot be broken

we weave through paths
and it becomes a testament to love
that never stops growing.

it reminds me of our walks to school
every morning and every afternoon
as the rhythm of our footsteps
create moments while the world awakens.

you are my vow,
my declaration of commitment
to never leave your side.

their laughter floats under autumn leaves
as we make memories with each step.

vibrant and full of life,
from tender touch to whispered words,
my love expands mile by mile.

i never thought i would experience
such magical moments.

being their father is the event of my life.

this will stay with me always

and i can embrace all the feelings
where rebirth and the spirit live.

i take away everything else that i am
and live fully in these moments,
majestically under the golden sun.

endurance

i hope these words endure
as the most beautiful homage
to the love
i have for you.

eyes with radiance,
faces with tranquility,
and the ancient majesty of our hearts
give me a sense of purpose,
to leave a lasting imprint on your souls.

you are my path
through stars and storms.

you are my testament
to all that is true
amidst the ever-present
passage of time.

among all the improbabilities
that prevailed over the chance
of nothingness and eternal night,
we are here together,
with wholeheartedness
and without any regret.

take comforts wherever
you can find them,
always make one last grasp
at light amidst the darkness.
remember that today or tomorrow
can be our last days,

so let's rest, but let's also live.
at the end of my life,

i will be able to smile with integrity
and heartbreaking humility
because i have known
love without bounds.

i have forgiven everything,
and i have spent my days knowing always

knowing,
who and what

was most important.

even now i want you
to come to me with prayerfulness,
lay your head on my chest,
feel it rise and fall
with each breath and each heartbeat.

make this our last tender moment together
and our best chance
of remaining fully human.

all of us will rise and cease.

all is temporary and will pass.

so don't ever attach to things,
only to those we love.

remember there are no foolish children
or wise elders,
it's actually the other way around.
there are only wise children
and foolish elders.

in wind and soil,

my love and spirit
will stay with you.

let's gaze at the lone star
against the boundlessness of the night sky.

the feeling of your hand in mine
is the only reassurance
i will ever need,
so let's never stop holding each other.

transcendent

in our final days,
our hearts and minds
are capable of making images
that help us make sense of it all.

the ineffable feeling of reverence,
the search complete for profound meaning and solace.

forget the productivity and activities
that preoccupy most people in life
and just turn toward those you love.

there is immortality in this love,
and that is precisely the exquisiteness
and grandness of our immortal substance,
which lies hidden from view,
and exists beyond time and space.

you are my wonder and majesty now.

before you,
i only found this in nature.

and it is this nature that reminds us
every day that nothing lasts.

so rest into this with calm acceptance.

it awaits us all, so live.

live life
with contemplation.

live life
finding words with meaning.

live life
with simplicity over complexity.

live life
moving forward if you can,
but moving backward is also fine.

live life
in its simplest and purest form,

and the infinite in time will be yours.

live life
with salvation,
bringing together the finite and the infinite.

live life
with the bittersweet beauty
of a deeply human rite of passage.

i think of you, my daughters,
only a few years ago,
and you were smiling with your missing teeth
and riding on the back of my bicycle.

the solitude of the night
is when i feel most connected
to the life of this world,
but nothing will ever replace
our shared reality of love and hope.

for my publisher

i had a late start as a published poet.

my first collection was published when i was 49,
though i have been writing poems since i was 13.

before publishing,
at the end of each year,
sometime in december,
i would gather the year's poems and stories
and make little books
printed out on looseleaf paper.

i would fold the paper in half,
take a 3-hole puncher to the left side,
and make the binding out of nature twine.

i gave the books to my family and friends.

and then, my 25-year-friendship
with marina changed everything.

opening the message:

> *"are you still writing…?*
> *i would love to publish your words.*
> *i created an independent press*
> *and i want yours to be the first book*
> *i publish."*

it was easy saying yes to marina.
she always had a great, beautiful stillness to her,
along with honest eyes and a pure soul.

then the poems i had been writing
all my life arrived for me.

and so in every moment, in every endeavor,
i have poured my unbreakable thread of love
into these words, pages, and books.

so i spend every night after my day job
writing with labor and with love.

and my day job gives me
a constant wonderment for life

as i work as a hospital administrator

and consider hospitals a sacred place,
for in what other profession can you come to work
where new life begins with the magic of birth
and old life exits with the lamenting of death,
and both occurring while you are "at the office?"

how is it that we can be safely here
among all of life one instant and then
irretrievably gone the next?

it is serious work during the day
and quiet reflection during night.

and because of this,
i am aware that the most beautiful thing
about day is that when it dawns,
there is always a sunrise after the night has passed.

i've always been unafraid to weep,
so i hold these tears and these words aloft at all times.

i know i will get greyer, and perhaps
my embrace will grow weaker and more trembly,
but i will always wrap my arms around you.

we may find ourselves fumbling and faltering,
but we will find our way through.

unyielding in patience and in presence,
the fleeting nature of this wakefulness
will leave a sense of amazement.

and i never have to worry about
finding out too late what is most essential.

finality

i will have no pain
and i only hope
that this absence in what is dying
is a beautiful gift for what is living.

the finality of tragedy and joy
that define great art,
also does the same with life.

i will only ever leave your side
against my raging and howling wishes.

but if i have to, i will do so
to accompany the gentle night,
and you will always find my heart
in the moon above, cradling the stars.

the final years

hoping the final years of my life
will be the most virtuous and purest
as i hold on to these
heart-clenching, vital,
and vulnerable moments,
shivering with love and suffering.

i stare at you with your
shining, piercing,
dazzling eyes
and i return to myself

and fall in love with you again
and with this now shimmering world,
which has loved us all for centuries.

perkins pancake house

eating a meal, a breakfast meal,
with my friend from high school
at 9pm on a friday night.

just two 18-year-olds enjoying a night out.
then there was a sudden shock.
something happened so violently
that i have remembered it all my life.

we finished eating
and made our way to the parking lot.

we were approached by two men
who grabbed us and put a gun to my face.

his friend said, "that's him—that's the driver.
he's the one we have to kill."
i was driving my friend's car,
so i immediately thought it was mistaken identity.

the man yelled at me to lie down
with my face to the ground.
he said, "kiss the dirt."

i got down and turned my face
and looked up to see the 1/2 moon,
and everything got very quiet.

i couldn't hear anything.

it was peaceful.

until i began thinking my life would end
in the parking lot of a pancake house.

i did hear the gun click,
but nothing happened.

i heard the guy say, "it's jammed."

his friend said, "try again."
it clicked again, but nothing.

he said, "beat him to death."

so he started hitting
the back of my head with the gun.

i kept my face to the left
so he couldn't break my nose
or have my teeth knocked out.

in between the beating,
i saw the 1/2 moon again:
it was my guide.
a couple came out of the pancake house
and the 2 guys got scared and ran away.

at first i was angry
and wanted to kill both of them,
but then i felt a hopeless sadness.

the powerlessness i felt about life
and my life consumed and confused myself,
and my 18 years.

it has never left me,

this sense of horror.

but i was able to take hold

of this experience and turn it
into a life-affirming event,
reminding me
to always stay present
and always know that it can end
in an instant at any moment.

the very next day,
i walked by the ocean,
the open air,
the majestic trees,
the naked fields,
the changes of seasons,
the sun during the day
the stars by night,

and i was renewed and restored
in body and in spirit.

my soul won't let me thank
the man with the gun,
but i was given the gift of presence

and gratitude at a young age.

and i have carried this with me all these years.

i always return to what is noblest,
which means most natural in us,

most deeply instilled,

which is time
and life and love.

stars

with fidelity to these final pages,
i would like to capture some of what
i have felt and what i have seen.

i sit here and look up at the night sky
to catch my usual glimpse of the stars,

and i know other stars are silently streaking
and perhaps falling and maybe finding their fates,
but these stars above are mine tonight and
they give me all the illumination needed.

in this tapestry of storylines beyond our control,
we can also refuse to resign ourselves
to surrendering.

and perhaps there is no final act for us
since we return to stardust anyway,
and we can watch ourselves through these stars
unfolding into the wonder of life.

capable

we live in a world capable of
trees and tenderness,
birds and poetry,
oceans and music,
clouds and painting,
snow and sculpture,
birth and passing.

and this life continues
with those we love
and they are here
to console us from
our human struggles
and allow for reawakening.

they make us remember
the importance of goodness and attention,
the dual sacraments for the spirit
to be bestowed on others
through our communion with nature
and our contemplation of art

as we meet beauty
on her own terms and timescales
and embrace our imperfections lovingly.

young love

the concept of kindness
is not easy to understand
because of so much human selfishness
surrounded by false certitudes.

we have to avoid the anxious
and the uncertain in us,
and make sure that poetry
doesn't become a self-obsession
filled with human vanity
that will only blind us to reality
and make us lie to ourselves,
telling us many stories that aren't true.

we need to look at
the human dimensions of life,
with arms outstretched,
and do everything we can
to keep those we love continuing always.

we need to look at life
with the eyes of young love
and share the infinite possibility
of the vows that we speak,
never making our words insignificant
and keeping our wholeness of character,
which will be reflected and refracted
through my eyes onto yours.

mortality

i don't stumble when i think about mortality.

i can vision not existing.

some famous writers and psychiatrists
have said that it's impossible to imagine our own death
and that every one of us is convinced of our immortality.

that is simply not true.

i have not felt this way since a very young age.

maybe because i have come very close to death
on a few occasions:

i have witnessed death in person at age 16
with the decapitation of a young mother
in front of her husband and 2 young daughters,

i have seen a man stabbed to death on the nyc subway.

i have seen a man crushed to death by a nyc subway car.

i have seen a motorcyclist hit and killed by a truck
and i have almost been killed at least 4 times:
gun put to my head with the trigger pulled
and the gun jammed,
gun pulled on me in an armed robbery in a nyc subway
knife showed to me on the nyc subway,
attempted carjacking with 11 bullets shot at
my car.

somehow i survived, without a scratch.

so i can imagine my death;

i know that i am not immortal.

what i hope remains is the love
i have shared for my daughters, my parents,
my brother, and a few beautiful others.

hoping this love remains
somehow in the spirit of life.

hoping these words i leave behind

capture what i have thought, what i have seen,

and what i have felt.

one day soon i will cease to be.

i am aware of the threats to my being each day,
this is a fact and a glaring possibility.

i am an impermanent human fated to a brief existence.

i embrace the breathlessly inevitable vulnerability in dying
as i approach my own finality without any terror.

the only thing that haunts me is this question:
why do we have to say goodbye to everyone we love at some point?

we have already shared the most moments
of life with such great love,
it almost can't be put into words.

i feel a little daily attrition of bodily dignity,
but i will not let this bleed into an attrition of character.

prayer and church, although comforting for many,

don't work for me as i know full well that these
so-called gods won't stop everything and grant wishes
because if that's so, they wouldn't have caused
all this pain in the first place and the countless
horrors visited on the world on a daily basis.

there is no one to answer to because there is no one there.

it's one of the great cruelties
and great glories of our very humanity,
and we will always find ourselves
torn between these two worlds.

my utterances have slowed, but my words on paper
have come at will, which is innate and essential
to my being and my heart.

i will hold the hands that move time,
i will breathe this glorious air,
and i will let these tears, always in my eyes,
weep while i sleep now in another world.

the result

the result of life is death and grief.
the result of love is loss and yearning.

yet we still live and love with an open heart
because this can merge the impossible with the eternal.

it can also become the aria of our lifetime.

and this will stay in our existence,
and our children's spirit,
and be left in each generation that follows us.

the miraculous

i touched the miraculous in this unbidden moment
with your love and felt a sense
that maybe there is another world beyond this one.

maybe it's the continuity of life across time,
where every day is an enlightenment
and where we live
with the absolute insistence
on the wonder of life.

rest

rest beneath a tree
with the warm sunlight
and look up at the pine needles
glistening in this same light
streaming through clouds and shadows.

i can see your love in this light
and i take it all in because
i will never see it again so beautifully presented.

i will never hear it again in notes so well put together.

i will never touch it again on the flesh of your skin.

but i will live with total wakefulness
and total openness
as i find myself in tears
at the thought of all the people
who came before me trying their best
to make the world a more divine place.

this history of life
is also the history of love.

so remember
we are, in some deep sense,
what we love.

so live and love now
and let your heart take over
with all its beautiful carelessness.

the lasts

we need to understand that the lasts
can indeed be the last.

your mother's embrace,
not knowing if it is the final farewell.

the lover you kiss,
not knowing if you will ever kiss again.

your father answering the phone in a voice
you've known your whole life,
a voice you don't know if you will ever hear again.

your children sleeping next to you,
breathing in and out,
the synchronicity of your heartbeats,
not knowing if you will
ever experience this wonder again.

so with the rising and unfolding of night,
feel your last feeling,
think your last thought,
hold your last embrace,
kiss your last kiss,
touch your last touch,
sing your last song,
and write your last poem.

as my mom would always say,
sleep well with angels on your pillow
through this silent symphony of eternity.

goodnight, my loves.

blink

pay compassionate attention to the world.

be fully awake to everything.

look at what is imperceptible to most eyes.

look for the subtlety.

look for the otherworldly.

look for the daily miracles,
like the clouds above
or wildflowers on a city street.

let your eyes be stunned into silence.

let your heart be paralyzed into stillness.

let life live through you.

grasp the fragility of sight and sound.

have hard-to-describe feelings
for the sea and the sky
and the love that is sitting next to you.

this is our humanness
and our vast reminder
to live in this blessed blink of existence.

it is our triumphant transcendence
that brings nothing but a sigh of relief.

revel in the joy
of this unexpected grace

as our souls are filled
with remarkable delight.

it is our lifetime of days.

still point

the crying shadow
and the loud lamenting
for the remarkable privilege
of running out of time,
of time past and time future.

should we follow the echoes we hear
as they emanate out to infinity?

you are my still point
in this turning, befallen world.

and we live in lovely times,
but life is lived through you
and the soul of your existence.

you make the timelessness
the essence of life.

for you are the assurance
of my own permanence
in a very impermanent universe.

you keep the clarity of my mind alive
with these memories and remembrances
that will not fade over time
and only illuminate
the unshakable poignancy of everyday life
and the wholeheartedness of everyday love.

be

be
remembered
and
time
is
conquered.

hold it first

don't let our lives become unwoven,
look for the echantment
that makes life worth living.

the history of humanity is filled
with those who withdraw their love
across the arrow of time.

we need a way to live with our human fragility,
beauty, and our interconnectedness.

let's embrace what has not yet been noticed
and what has not yet been named.

let's call it a fragment of what you felt,
of what you knew to be true,
before anyone else realized the same.

more precious was your laughter and your love,
and i had the privilege of an absolute stunning miracle
to hold it first in the most exquisite, invisible way,
with hidden golden threads weaving my heart together.

always remain

i see the horizon hovering
where the sea meets the sky
and i know our course is marked by the stars.

the sounds of nature and silence
wash over me whenever i am near you.

i think about you even when we are together,
and you will never be more than i can hold,
and you will never weigh me down.

i stand outside myself and look at you,
my eyes burning with tears,
but i can still see the colored lights
through the grey clouds.

let me enfold you,
because there is no lovelornness between us.

in this midnight blue,
please lie next to me
and let's forget the world.

with words unspoken,
i hold a silent devotion for you.

the end will always come too soon,
but what a day to start anew,
and what a day to start breathing.

you will never be forgotten
for your bones will always
have a place to rest.

your words still echo through my home.

i know how many freckles you have on your face.

i know everything about you.

to be acknowledged by your hands makes me want to cry.

and i am sorry i cry, but i just break that way.

i know that this world was never meant

for someone as beautiful as you.

you have been the only thing that's right
in all i've done.

this is our ethereal place,
where our openhearted love
belongs to us and it remains unbounded.

please remember that you are
the evidence of my life,

and the holding of you
will always remain
with the urgency of now.

meaningfulness

we shine as gloriously as we are able
and then we are gone,
but our essence will be revealed.

in the face of this impermanence,
it takes courage to love,
but this will yield an expansion of our being.

we become what we love anyway,
so the song to be sung is perhaps
a beautiful requiem for our irreplaceable losses.

some people give the human race
a real reason to be proud,

terrible things happen in life,
but love always steps in
and makes repairs serenely and eternally.

find value in the retelling,
in the slow sharing of our lives,
marking in ink both the joys
and the heartbreaks.

the acceptance that our time is limited,
but our possibilities are limitless.

the uniqueness of our existence in this world
of every day,
of every hour,
of every moment
as our whole life stands
in the face of death
to our very last breath
with harmonious vitality.

exist

every love is different.

no love is ever wasted,

even if it is unrequited,

even if it leads to heartbreak,

even if it ends in betrayal,

even if it was imaginary.

i repeat: no love is ever wasted.

just find the people
you want to be around and be around them.

love them wholeheartedly,
accepting each other's missteps
and celebrating your imperfections.

marvel at the good fortune
of finding each other.

the staggering improbability
that you met is only surpassed
by the inexplicable caring
you have for one another.

your love can transform the ephemeral
into something permanent.

your love can change the mortal
into something eternal.

everything beautiful
that you have in this world:
birdsong,
sunsets,
kisses,
poems,
songs,
is a bittersweet reminder
of what will eventually be lost.

and if it all ends,
the love still remains
because there is always something
that remains of the life we once lived.

grief is real because the love was real.

grief means you remember.

and grief gives you the fortitude
to continue living and loving.

as with all matters of the heart,
you'll know when you find it.

all the love you once poured into them still exists.
it will always exist, just like an eternal poem.

my children are my teachers

my children have taught me
everything about life.

i see the innumerable things they learn
and how much they risk,

how they try and fail sometimes,
and how they are never defeated.

i will never punish any of their failures.

i tell them every day:
please don't worry
about your grades in school.

it doesn't matter.
do your best,
and don't worry about failing.
it's not that important in life.

the definitions our society places
on what brings "success" are just not true.

and certainly not worth it.

there is always beauty
in the possibility for renewal,
for starting again,
after an unsuccessful attempt.

the inevitable incompletion
of human life is quite special.

it is the shining and the seeing.

there is actually no failing in life
other than not being able
to be kind or to love.

kindness and love
are the only substance of true achievement.

that is your success.

we will never forget the sweetness

and the enchanted world of childhood,
and we will fully understand
what those days of joy contain.

know that i spend
all my days and nights with you,
even when we are not together.

the courageous part
is loving you so much,
even though at some moment
i know i will have to say goodbye.

you are now
and always will be
my portal and threshold of wonder
for every single dimension
of my existence.

this is our inheritance:

the beauty before us,
human heart to human heart,
rare and startling,
sweeping and magnificent.

and our intimate invitation
to breathe together
with the trees,
with the clouds,
and with each other.

life and time

life will always sweep us off course:

through accidental sightings,
through a new love that enters our heart,
through a diagnosis,
through a loved one lost.

life shows us again and again
there is no certainty,
and no settled way of being.

we have to find beauty in uncertainty
and completeness in being unsettled.

that is where our hope lies waiting.

this is our sacred time,
our time to touch the ineffable
by loving each other.

our time to make
our past and our future
our living present.

keeping our souls vibrantly alive
is our gift to give.

i want to feel it all,
to stay ablaze with emotion
because the ensuing beauty,
and all its tragedy have been exquisite.

your eyes

even in the face of catastrophe,
there's solace to be found
in the immense depth of your eyes
and in your redemptive whispered words.

you are simply the wellspring
of my singular humanity.

our small acts

saying please and thank you,

asking if someone ordered already
when standing in line for coffee,

holding the door for each other,

pulling your feet in when someone walks by,

letting the other car merge in front of you,

saying 'bless you'

opening a taxi door for someone,

carrying a heavy bag for someone,

remembering their birthday,

writing a love letter,

sending a handwritten note of thanks,

making the bed,

all enhancing the way you live your life,
**which in turn will widen out
the boundaries of your being**
as you keep intense immersion
and a sense of clarity
when you realize the time,

and feel like you're part of something
much larger than yourself.

this will be your blueprint
to a life of meaning.

so go about your day,
but see the world
with absolute honesty
and sympathetic perception,

remembering when you heard that
piece of music that made you cry

or recall the flutter of your heart
as you stared at the delicate soul
across from you in that restaurant.

take it all in:
the contemplation
and the consecration,
the glory
and the grief.

the virtues of having
a breathable heart
are immeasurable,

because you can
transfer tenderness
and practice possibility
all with atemporal insight
into the urgency of being.

last line written

nature can be found
in the forest
and on a beach,
but it can also be found
on a city sidewalk.

wherever we are,
that is where nature is too.

it is here.

we just have to notice it.

my last line written
will always be one of pure love
and gratitude for this life.

you

i don't want to be anywhere
that isn't close to you.

if i only had a few more hours to be in love,
i would want to live them with you only.

i hope i can teach you that the world is full of love
amidst the ancient temples and sacred sites.

our astounding love will magnify
the smallest details of life
and bring endless joy
through the cycle of light and rebirth,
where the losses are restored
in the shadow of the moon.

we live ever more harmoniously
as we compose a hymn to time,
without ever mourning the life
we were not meant to share.

and remember,
if our lives were novels,
we would certainly pick
the same epigraph to begin our stories.

turtle music
(for mia)

sleeping next to my 9-year-old daughter, mia.

first, she puts on the tv
and goes to calming, meditative
music of turtles swimming in the ocean
as the universe sings to us.

she lays on her back
with her eyes closed.

i take my thumb and middle finger
and start touching in between her eyebrows
and rub outward, stopping at her temples
to make circular motions.

i listen for her breathing,

which becomes more pronounced,
and she falls asleep within 5 minutes.

i lie there
and listen to her breathing,
the slow music in the background,
the turtles swimming…

i put my hand on her back
and close my eyes to this glorious night.

the sunset

the sunsets i will never forget
as long as i live.

the colors:
red,
then orange,
and then yellow,
with a hint of blue.

part spiritual,
part beautiful.

the emotion of the moment
fills me with all i need
as i watch with my 2 daughters
and my mother by my side.

the eclipse
(monday, april 6, 2024)

the movement of the moon's shadow,
shimmering and still,
blocked out the sun,
and darkness covered the light of day
as the clouds hung close to the horizon.

a hushed calm ensued
under a promising sky
as the sun became one with the moon
and a halo glowed proudly.

it was our magical moment
of childlike wonder and awe.

in the face of the profound,
with these rare feelings,
i think we both felt a privilege
to be in this presence.

this was our elegant opportunity
to be part of the greater story.

the transcendent reverence
of the spiritual and science
wrapped in one moment
where the delicate equilibrium
coexists in harmony and unified balance.

the eclipse is available
to all humans and animals,
and even all things,
showing us the complexity
of the universe,
which is really an offering

to the mystery
we find ourselves living in.

think about this-
even the stones on the ground
will cool when the sun disappears,
the leaves on the trees
will not get their photosynthesis.

this is our mirror,

reflecting our beliefs
among this universal connectedness.

but it's not just the eclipse on this day…

i look up at the stars
and the moon every night,
catch as many sunsets
and sunrises as i can,

and am in awe almost all the time

and fully understand that we are part
of something much larger.

it should be every day and every night
that we feel this presence.

i wish the masses gathering today
would realize that.

it's about being present
to the moment,
to the world,
and to those we love,
standing right next to us.

the eclipse itself
and for that matter,
all events in life,
isn't what matters,

but rather who we are with to share the wonder
of how the sun and the moon come together
to offer us an enchanting shadow
on our miraculous planet
so full of life and love.

aliveness

our emotions are the only things
that give us meaning
for the brief time we are here together,

as we celebrate the wonder of this world,
which is always unfinished and bittersweet,

with the ephemeral and the eternal
bridging harmony across human divides.

we can add to our staggering
sense of belonging
and the beauty of it all
as we celebrate our aliveness.

as we move through the stages of life,
the only way to do this right
is to meet each on its own terms,
and to honor the unfolding of time.

the person staring back at you from the mirror
has to be the one filled with tender gentleness
and an unquenchable joy of living.

count to 10

let's love
and hold it close.

let's close our eyes
and count to 10.

i will always be here waiting
to touch you for this blink of time.

you are my human hymn
of praise for humankind
and you are the most beloved of all.

in this most rare hour,
the first words arise
and they are always for you.

i hope you still hear these words
and my voice inside when i'm not here anymore.

the bereaved will find a way
from grief to fulfillment
and in all the joy that remains.

there are always pathways out of confusion.

and your emboldened hearts
will stay golden,
full of hopes and dreams.

life is better

the way you can love something
so dearly because it's leaving or changing.

we can only hope
that all human beings
are safe and sound in their homes,
cared for and beloved,
and all wars have ended.

we can huddle under streetlamps
or under those oak trees
and talk about how
life is better with silence,
or the sounds of nature,

and the slow beating of your heart.

writing

try
to
make
your
hand
write
the
words
that
you
feel,
without
having
to
think
of
your
hands.

burst of emotion

bound by time and place
in the dark,
my feet search for something real.

i drift to you under these sheets
and your words are all i hear.

and i wonder if these words
are speaking from a future.

these rare moments
are what shines through
the fractures of daily life.

with this astonishingly graceful
burst of emotion,
your love removes all else
and reveals life's truest form
on the edge of possibility.

you are all the things
i reach for in life
against the deepening of the sky
as the moon slowly shows her glowing ring.

in the vast open emptiness
of these infinite horizons,
we can remain the great souls of our time.

these star-lit nights
on grass-covered lawns
radiating from beauty
are also a glorious elegy
because it is our life's story,
which will survive through these centuries.

sacred feelings

a portrait of sacred feelings
and a purity of heart, undimmed.

we sit in the house and watch
the windows breathing in the light,
with a timeless serenity,
as we reflect on the delicacy
of giving and receiving love.

immense grace

unburdened from the opinion of others,
social agendas, and work events,

take a rest from responsibilities
and take a magnificent glimpse
at your luminous spirit,
and let it breathe with aloneness
into your sacred solitude.

this is fiercely necessary.

this is the most consistently enchanting way
to live with your secret knowledge,
and the courage to be yourself,

to live with unassailable integrity,
great simplicity, and unpretentious sincerity,

to honor and endure the value of being human
and all that could be seen in the present moment.

embrace the miraculously beautiful things
we spend our whole lives looking for,
getting lost to be found,
and staying lost in her arms
lost to the world.
looking at the grandeur of earth,
take in our smallness,
and let your undivided day and night linger
with reflections of the immense grace of your love.

not to be sold

i have always viewed
my words and books
as something
to be published, not sold.

i view them all
as small, miraculous elegies
and memorials to life and love.

wakeful dreaming
(thursday, april 11, 2024)

walking into my ex-wife's apartment
to wake up my daughters
to get them ready for school.

i hit the button for the elevator
and start crying.

right there in the lobby.

i am present with full emotion
and the fidelity of feeling.

this is our tender tale
about the meaning of life
as we stay close with exquisite sensitivity
and pause to take in our moments
of reflection and illumination
with our wakeful dreaming together.

the glory of this all will never be lost on me.

my day job

fortunately, there is no money in poetry,
so to pay the bills i work in healthcare,
for a hospital in manhattan.

i was raised by what i call "healers,"
so it was a natural fit.

my grandfather was a primary care physician,
my father was a surgical oncologist,
my mother was a pediatric nurse,
and my brother is a reconstructive and plastic surgeon.
i remember the transcendent moments
of sitting together for dinner
and listening to their stories,
which were always heart wrenching,
and yet incredibly inspiring.

i learned early on that healthcare is not a job,
but an obligation.

i like the seriousness and responsibility
that comes with a job where when you come to work,
someone is born and someone dies.

the humility needed to play a part
in a person's life for a moment
and in their family's life even longer
is an honor and a delightful burden.

we move through the world yearning for harmony and peace
so we can live with consciousness and composure.

all i ask is that i am granted
some temperance,
some tranquility,

and some humility
as i witness and observe what makes this life bearable
as something greater that vanquishes the self
and returns us to the miracle of life
and the magnificence of the here and now.

poetry

is poetry something we make
or something we are made of?

sometimes i ask these words
to hold what i cannot hold.

the words remain in my head
mercifully, blessedly silent.

we live in a city and a country
where no one seems to get along anymore
or even talk to one another.

so let's try living with presence
through and of these words,
and maybe it becomes a bridge of harmony
across human divides as they anchor us
in the grandeur of our existence.

my words for you
unfold as one breathless whisper
from my mouth to yours,
stitched together with echoes
of all who loved here before us
with pure generosity of heart and spirit.

ordinary things

the heartbreaking simplicity
of ordinary things:

bits of wood,
grains of sand,
shells and pebbles,
tiny flowers,
falling leaves,
sunrises and sunsets,
clouds moving,
tides ebbing and flowing,
sitting in the garden,

our soulful invitations
to the joy of being alive.

we continue with the full awareness
that these moments will become memories.

so please move ahead toward happiness
and wholeness with rivers of emotion.

it's a quiet amazement that we exist at all.

ask yourself again:

how do you want to live
for the brief time we have together
on this lonely, yearning planet?

perhaps the overwhelming immersion
into the understanding of the ephemerality of life
because our time here is short and precious.

we can hold the history

of our search for meaning,
as we stay still and stay solemn
with our intriguing and elusive
love for life and for each other.

secrecy

the secrecy of our smiles
dissolves into the air
as afternoon turns into evening

and the single question of life
still has the best answer

which is always love.

works of art

i gaze upon you
like a work of art,

but you are so beautiful
that most other works of art
are rendered completely irrelevant.

haunting and comfortable

the inexplicable weight of your heart
is always vulnerable
to the accidents of our universe.

this is both haunting and comforting.

circumstances can overturn
in an instant with little more
than a single word,
a message left,
a note received.

but we are alive and breathing
and our love stretches all the way back
to the beginning of what shaped our life.

and this is our exquisite destiny.

sunset and weeping
(sunday, april 14, 2024, 7:30pm)

driving with you back to manhattan,
the sun started to set
behind the boundless clouds
and i started to weep.

you went into the glove compartment
and handed me a tissue without a word
and held my hand.

that was all.

a perfect way to end the day
amidst our daily devotion to each other.

22,630 days

tenderly longing for your affection
the sheer astonishment i have
watching your eyes change color
under the sun's light
allows me to harmoniously
cross this river of life

as i realize the shining example
of my parents' love
and how that love
remained and unfolded
upon me every minute
of every single day
as they were together
for a total of 62 years
or 22,630 days.

this splendor continues to expand between us.

you are the great gift of my life.

let's stay tenderhearted with serene awareness
as we behold each other until the end of time.

last love

one day you will eat your last meal,
smell your last flower,
hug your loved one for the last time.

so each day know your purpose.

and it's pretty simple:

the meaning of our lives
is nothing more than
great, redeeming love,

the kind of love that stays with you
for your entire lifetime,
finding its way into every aspect of your life,
whether consciously or unconsciously.

it's nothing more than the ancient
and abiding gift of the human heart.

hope

the seed sprouted

watching it blossom now
into a breathtaking flower
allows you to hold the possibilities
of this world in both hands.

it is the weaving together of many threads
through the profound quest for understanding
and the hope of hearing
those 3 words spoken to you alone
in the middle of the night.

and the flowers turn their faces towards the sun

childhood is our reminder
that we should remain unaware of time
and its relentless unfolding.

have the heart of a giant.

it is the effortless effort of our little ones.

start small and grow tall.

try not to actually "try,"

like children making art
with unselfconscious abandon,
creating things with their whole being.

we all know this world is capable
of bone-crushing brutality and daily cruelties.

don't ever allow the sunrise to leave you unmoved.

keep uncontainable gratitude for your very existence.

have no desire for perfection.

have no desire for awards,
those strange little monuments to the individual.

you learn nothing from winning.

it's in losing where you learn how to survive.

lose and lose again

in order to recover and rise
as you reach for greatness.

living in the world
in this expanded way
will be your permanent gift.

the simple act of goodness
and small gestures,
are the measure of your days.

look for the daily moments of kindness.

they will carry the weight of hope for you
and the sweet burden of love.

and you will always find it here
waiting for you as the earth moves

and
the
flowers
turn
their
faces
toward
the
sun.

postscript

some words that helped ...

A Thankful Poem
By Emma Silich, age 11, written on September 30, 2024

Thankful for my family.

Happy to be together.

Always food on the table.

Never sad, always thankful.

Kind to others.

Family and friends are always full of love.

Unity among everyone.

Love to be talking and laughing.

Words from Mia
by Mia Silich, age 9, written on December 17, 2024, Mia age 9

I just wanted to tell a very special secret

To a very special person:

I love you so much and thank you
for being the best dad in the whole world.

I love you so much!!!

See you tomorrow.

Acknowledgements

Once again, I would like to thank my publisher, Marina Aris, and the Brooklyn Writers Press for publishing this collection.

And again, Marina, thank you for your loyalty and trust, and of course, our over 25-year-friendship filled with kindness, tenderness, and understanding.

And for the words you sent me on July 31, 2024:

"I'm thrilled to publish your books. As time passes, this work is becoming much more meaningful to me too. I think we'll be able to make this all work. Thanks for always being so supportive and patient. This is wonderful."

I would like to thank my editor, Judi Heidel, for her always gentle touch that has provided guidance and inspiration from the first book to this latest.

I would like to thank:

My daughters, Emma and Mia,

Emma, thank you for the words you sent me on my birthday, April 30, 2023:

"Dear my wonderful dad. You are the best. You work so hard to take care of us. Thank you for everything. Happy Birthday! You also try so hard to make great food. You are my rainbow. I love you to the moon and back. I love you so much. Love, Emma"

Mia, thank you for the words you sent me on my birthday also, April 30, 2023:

"Dear Daddy. I love you so much. You are the best. Happy birthday! I hope you have an amazing birthday. The world is better when you are holding us tight. Since you are a poet, here is a poem:

"Roses are red, Violets are blue, Daisy's are sweet and so are you."

You are an amazing dad, and I will never forget you or your caring about other people. I hope you know how much I love you. You are the best dad in the world. I love you. Love, your Mia"

My dad, Robert Silich, I love you and miss you every day.

And for the words you sent me on April 30, 1991:

"Stephan, you are everything a parent could ever hope for in a son. Your considerate, caring nature, your honesty, and your sense of humor - all of this, and so much more, makes a parent proud. Hope you know how much you're loved - and how great it is having a wonderful son like you. Your mom and I are extremely proud of how you have grown to become an outstanding man. Love, Dad."

My mom, Dianne Silich, and the words she wrote me on July 12, 2006:

"Stephan, There is always a rainbow. Trust me. I wish you knew how scared Daddy and I were when we started out. We had no money and 2 kids. Then your dad got drafted. Somehow, things were simpler then. Money wasn't so important to us. Love was. Just hang in there and you will find your place somewhere. I am always right. Wait until you go to the party this weekend and you see some more crazies, I am sure. Just hang in there. Lots of love from me to you always, your Mom"

My brother, Robert Silich, thank you for the words you sent me on May 10, 1996:

"A few words to collect my thoughts of you. What a strange year for us both - love and loss, joy and pain dealt us both evenly. Yet I feel no real pain in the face of my one truth in life: my brother, myself. We share the same cells from the bottom to the top, and a bond of love and fate that our life's loves – whoever they may be – will never much as make a mark. I always envision my death scene with a flurry of memories of both of us: snowmobiling upstate New York, the phone call from American law school when you were in college, countless nights in D.C., rollerblading in the streets, vacations, and both of us crying – alone and together. You are the rock I break myself upon – solid – unwavering – ironic that you are so solid, yet you have always cared so little for the things that society values as marks of solidity. Anyway, just a few words after 27 years. I've never been kind to words as you are, but sometimes we scratch down these marks only to give a clue (never to really express, impossible as you know) a clue to the infinite realm of love we all have, we all possess, and the infinite realm of love we will always live with. I love you, Stephan. Always did, always will. Robert"

Joanne Megna, thank you for the words you sent me on February 23, 1994:

"Dear Stephan, Just a little note to thank you for allowing me to read your poetry. It seemed to be such a personal journey, changing and maturing beautifully. To translate your emotions and conceptualize your thoughts into verse is an art. To me, a poet bears his soul and, in doing so, shares the innocence and the complexities that form the collage that is his life. He can only hope that in this vulnerable state he is understood and can touch that common core that ties us all together. Your poetry touched me. I hope one day to read more. Fondest regards, Joanne Megna."

Rita Wu thank you for the words you sent me on August 23, 2001:

"The resolve to write this letter is in no sense trivial, given the circumstances. I intend it to supplant a dialogue we never had. After all, I let many months elapse without ever finding the opportunity to tell you in person how much I enjoyed your poetry, and how meaningful it was to discover a kindred spirit in the beautiful verses you wrote. I was struck by the maturity of your feelings and the simplicity of your eloquence. To read is to live life vicariously, but to write is the real thing. The latter demands a much daring passion and requires sacrifice and devotion. I admire your spirit of perseverance and your efforts to indulge always in your poetic voice. You have chosen a path inconvenient to financial rewards, and clearly incongruous with the communal urge to chase material merrymaking.

A poet rarely fails to nourish a suffering soul at the expense of his own agony. You have certainly inspired me. The rugged path you chose has deposited you to an often-lonely climb. I pray that the blessings of chance will be bestowed along with your literary way, and you are kept company by those few who share your conviction and endure your perseverance. You have an audience, and a rooter in me. Yours always, Rita Wu."

Jennifer Fontao, thank you for the words you wrote me on October 31, 2020:

"I told the stars about you. You are a most unique, creative, and spectacular being. Thank you for being born. I couldn't have invented you, even if I wanted to. I first saw you in the distance through the dirty double-glass doors. I squinted, wishing they were cleaner. You found my smile in the longest moments between the seconds. You are a beautiful writer, son, father, and friend to all of those lucky enough to know the real you. Jennifer"

For the others, the very few others, I know who you are, thank you for the privilege of loving you and being loved.

About the Author

Stephan Silich, an award-winning poet and storyteller, masterfully interweaves art, literature, and the diverse landscapes of New York's iconic streets. His collections seamlessly blend vibrant and mundane moments of lived experience with the intricacies of human emotion, crafting a rich lyrical tapestry that resonates deeply with poetry lovers.

Born into a family of healers, Silich's work is infused with a profound sense of compassion and empathy. His father, a surgical oncologist, his mother, a pediatric nurse, and his brother, a plastic and reconstructive surgeon, all influenced his unique perspective on the human experience.

Silich's journey as a writer began at 13, inspired by his parents' encouragement and shaped by his brother Robert's advice:

"If it sounds like writing, then rewrite it. Sometimes your poetry is the victim of poetry. Just write from your heart and the words will beautifully arrive."

This counsel has guided Silich's approach, resulting in critically acclaimed collections that speak directly to the heart.

His debut, *The Silence Between What I Think and What I Say* (2018), earned praise from Kirkus Reviews.

> *"Silich slips effortlessly into a long tradition of New York poets from Walt Whitman to Frank O'Hara and his poems are a delight."*
>
> —Kirkus

His second collection, *Tonight Will Be the Longest Night of Them All*, was a finalist in the prestigious 2021 Next Generation Independent Book Awards. Subsequent collections, *Putting the Trembling Kiss at Ease* (2023) and *Remember Me as a Time of Day* (2024), also received critical acclaim and have further cemented his reputation for evocative and lyrical prose.

Praised for over two decades for his vulnerability and contemplative candor, Silich's work offers a unique form of poetic medicine that soothes the soul and mends the spirit. His blend of memoir and introspection invites poetry lovers to explore how human emotions and human experience converge. Many of his devoted readers claim his perspective on the recurring themes in his work, namely: family, love, loss, art, literature, and creative muses, such as his native New York have transformed them.

Silich divides his time between Manhattan and East Hampton, where he lives with his two daughters, Emma and Mia. He continues to write daily, with several collections in progress, solidifying his place as a significant voice in contemporary American poetry.

www.ingramcontent.com/pod-product-compliance
Lightning Source LLC
Chambersburg PA
CBHW070134080526
44586CB00015B/1689

Thank You for Reading
And the Flowers Turned Their Faces Toward The Sun
by Stephan Silich

If you enjoyed reading this book, please consider leaving a review on your preferred platform. Your feedback supports quality content and helps inspire future releases.

Connect with the Author
 @stephan_silich

Want more from the Brooklyn Writers Press?
Browse our complete catalog.

brooklynwriterspress.com